Millionaire Habits:

Financial Advice For

"Thousandaires"

First Edition

Fess Crockett

To My Bride,

I love you with all my heart! Your encouragement is fantastic!

Love,

Your Groom

To My Children,

Lily, Grace, and Hope, learn the fundamentals. Practice the fundamentals. Make the fundamentals a habit.

Love,

Your Daddy

Why I Wrote This Book

Who does not want to have more money? Most people would like to worry a lot less about their financial situation. My experience and training has allowed me to help the wealthy accumulate more and worry less. My ability to help the wealthy has been fun, exciting, but not completely fulfilling. I was not satisfied just helping a small number of fantastic clients, and four events that occurred within four weeks caused me to re-evaluate my life.

As president of a wealth management firm that caters to millionaires, I thoroughly enjoy helping my clients grow and preserve their net worth. My original goal was to create a firm that provided unparalleled service to a small number of wealthy clients. While pursuing this goal, there were a few events that occurred that challenged my original thinking and served as a catalyst to the creation of Fundamental Financial Advisors and this book. I realized that my ideas and financial methods should be shared with many others who, while they might not be millionaires, would greatly benefit from my approach. I then determined that I would start a new firm that serves "thousandaires", using the same wealth growing techniques I use to help millionaires. Here are the four events that launched me in the new direction:

- o "Why don't the good financial planners pay attention to people like me instead of just the wealthy?" This life changing question was asked by a friend of mine when he saw me walk out of the office of one of my multi-millionaire clients. I wondered to myself when I got back to my office, "Why aren't I helping people like my friend, instead of just the affluent?" My desire became to help others who know they need my help, but can't afford my rates.

- o A friend of my wife came over to our house. She shared with me the goal for her family to move beyond just "getting by" and moving toward creating a sizeable nest egg. My desire became to put my planning expertise to use for typical families who want to improve their financial well-being to "beyond typical".

- A member of my church came to visit me in my office. He talked about how something always was coming up that kept him from adding to his savings. He had a limited net worth and was not even contributing all he could to his 401k. I felt so guilty when I said that my firm was not oriented to people in his financial situation. My desire became to help families with average incomes increase their savings and net worth.

- The fourth event was an observation of how people with a typical net worth are treated by the financial planning industry. Most financial advisors I knew who were targeting typical families were selling mutual funds with a sales charge or commission, while the financial planners who helped the wealthy charge fees, not commissions. I thought the commission approach may not be oriented toward ongoing service, since these clients did not have large re-occurring purchases. My desire became to change the service to people who have a typical net worth so that they can pay a smaller fee and receive great service throughout the year, not just when they were about to "buy something".

These desires led to the building of Fundamental Financial Advisors and this book. Our goal for this book and Fundamental Financial Advisors is to help you act like a millionaire by:

- Better controlling your spending
- Increasing your ability to save more money
- Developing a well-researched investment plan
- Creating a lifetime financial plan

All at an affordable cost!

Contents

Keys to Budgeting

❖ Software makes it easier

❖ First analyze current spending

❖ Set goals even if you have to guess

❖ Monitor spending versus goals and
  brainstorm ways to cut costs at least
  twice a year

❖ Develop a new budget each year

Chapter One: Controlling Your Expenses

"Misers aren't much fun to live with, but they make great ancestors." – Anonymous

"A house is just a place to keep your stuff while you go out and get more stuff." - George Carlin

I had a friend who went out and purchased a new car that "blew" his budget. When I asked him about the extravagance, he simply replied that he just needed to have something "more shiny". Advertisers and marketing firms love people because we like the "shiny", we like the "sizzle". We like stuff …until the credit card bill arrives.

Controlling expenses is like going on a diet. We know what we need to do; we just don't always follow our own rules. There is not much new to a diet …eat less…exercise more…etc. Having more money is no different …spend less…save more…invest well. The problem is that while both sound easy, they are actually hard to do! This book will lay out what you need to do, and if you find it hard, I started a company called Fundamental Financial Advisors that will work with you and help you accomplish your financial goals!

Curbing spending habits can be extremely advantageous. A wise friend of mine married recently. At his rehearsal dinner he talked about how when friends tried to set him up with a potential girlfriend, he used to ask "What does she look like?", but now that he was wiser he asked, "Is she frugal?"

Keeping overhead low while keeping your priorities at the forefront can help build wealth. I am not saying be cheap, but be frugal. Spend more money on appreciating assets, like a home, and less on depreciating assets. Splurging at times may make sense, but "living high on the hog" can bring ruin.

Curbing your spending can be accomplished using a five-point plan:

1. Track your actual spending
2. Develop spending goals
3. Analyze your spending against your goals twice a year
4. Brainstorm how to reduce your spending based on the above analysis
5. Change your goals yearly to reflect the changes in your lifestyle

Step One. A report that tracks how you spend your money can be an eye opener! Think of a spending report as a scale – it doesn't lie, it can be ugly, but it can help you achieve your goals. Tracking your spending is a lot easier than it used to be. Technology has come a long way in this area to make keeping track of your spending fairly easy and does not require a lot of time.

Online banking, budget-oriented websites (such as Mint.com) and computer programs (such as Quicken) are some of the computer programs that will save you a lot of time. Many of these programs can access your bank and credit card records and update your records on a regular basis with a "touch of a button". Once you have "linked" your bank accounts and credit card accounts to the budgeting software, you can create spending reports that reveal how you spend your money.

If you are not tech savvy our firm, Fundamental Financial Advisors helps our clients use these websites.

Step Two. The spending report dissects your purchases into categories that reveal your spending preferences. The revealing reports show your spending in total as well for various categories like groceries, home repair, etc. With this knowledge you can establish spending goals.

Look at the data in the spending report. Often the first report will only have about three months of data. Then estimate what you think your annual spending will be (in total and for each category). This estimate in scientific terms is called an "educated guess". The point is to develop a goal even if you are not that sure of its accuracy. The spending report will help, and your financial advisor may be a good resource to take a few months of your data and then develop a forecast or budget for the rest of the year. Once you have a full year of data, the process becomes much more accurate.

Step Three. After your goals are determined, you will need to assess your spending versus your goals. The newer software programs produce spending reports that help in this assessment. They show your actual spending versus your goals and highlight the differences.

Step Four. While the spending reports are helpful and provide a fact base for discussion, the real value is in the evaluation of the reports. At least twice a year your actual spending versus goals should be reviewed and ways to cut costs should be brainstormed. Pay careful attention to those categories where your expenses are over ten percent of your goal. Discussions should be focused on how to reduce these "greater than expected" costs.

During your expense review, you can understand if your spending priorities are consistent with your savings priorities. You may even decide to create a category called "savings". The idea is to evaluate how you can reduce expenses in order to save more for the future.

Step Five. Each new year you should review your actual spending levels by category and create a new budget with new goals. Every time you create a new budget, you will be able to more accurately forecast your expenses. You should also be in a better position to understand the lifestyle trade-offs between spending now and saving for later.

Keys to Saving More Money

❖ Understand the value of compounding interest

❖ Make the commitment

❖ Determine how much you want to save each year

❖ Substitute, reduce, eliminate

❖ Pay yourself first

❖ Create a separate savings/investment account

Chapter Two: Saving More Money

"I put a dollar in a change machine, but nothing changed." – George Carlin

Don't we all wish it would be easy to make positive changes to our life? Change can be hard, but the payoff can be great! Unfortunately to save more money you have to change your habits, so please keep the future great benefits in the front (not the back) of your mind.

Have you heard the expression, "Having money can burn a hole in your pocket"? A friend of mine saved money by sticking to his budget and I commented about how excited I was about his efforts. He responded, "I better invest it quick because I don't trust myself. If the money is close by, I will spend it." This money was burning a hole in his pocket!

One time my bride made the comment, "Why don't we use our money to buy things we want, rather than always depositing it in a bank". I responded, "That's why it is called *savings* and not *spendings*". She laughed at that comment and has repeated it throughout our financial discussions.

To increase your savings, I recommend a four-step plan:

1. Make a commitment to save more.
2. Develop a savings goal.
3. Substitute, reduce, and eliminate some of your purchases.
4. Automatically deduct your savings from your checking account and deposit the money in an investment account.

Step One. I have stated that positive change is hard, so let's try to make it easier. Making a commitment to save more may be easier if you can understand the "magic" of compounding interest. Even if you can't understand it, it still can be a motivator! Basically the idea is that a dollar saved today is worth two dollars in the future.

Through the "magic" of compound interest your savings will grow faster and faster over time since the interest you earn in one year also earns interest in later years. For example you would earn $1000 interest on an original deposit of $10,000 if interest rates were 10%. If you keep all the money in the bank for another year, then that $1000 would also earn interest ($100) and the original $10,000 would earn interest (another $1000) for a total interest payment of $1100. While that $100 of "extra" interest may not seem like a lot of money, over time it can make a huge difference.

Each dollar saved today can create many more dollars to spend later in life. A steady savings plan can result in a sizeable nest egg by retirement. Also, given that people are living longer, it is never too late to begin to increase your savings. For example, a sixty year old may have over thirty years of time to see the effects of compounding interest.

Make the commitment to save more.

Step Two. Determine how much savings is reasonable. Saving for the future requires some sacrifice for today's spending. This sacrifice is not easy, especially in today's environment of consumerism, easy credit, and constant commercials enticing us to spend today.

My suggested process of determining your savings amount is by examining the two sides of the issue and working toward the middle. First, estimate how much money you will need to have when you stop working, and how much savings you will need to supplement social security and your retirement benefits. This is an involved exercise that will be discussed thoroughly in Chapter Four.

Second, start with the goal of saving twenty percent of your salary. This may be an optimistic goal, but it is a good starting point.

Third, compare the amount you will need to save for retirement with a twenty percent reduction in spending and develop a reasonable savings goal.

Step Three. Reductions to existing spending and the resulting increase in savings usually come in three areas (your financial advisor may be a good resource to use in identifying expenses in each of the three areas):

o   The first area is substitution and can be the least painful way to reduce expenses. Buy the same goods (but not always the same brand) from a cheaper supplier. An example of this is paying less for the same item at a discount store than you would at a more convenient retail store.

o   The second area of reduction (which can cause some pain) is reducing your consumption of a discretionary expense. An example of this would be eating at home more, instead of going out to a restaurant.

o   The third area is eliminating consumption, which can be the most painful. Here is where you examine your habits and determine where you can do without. An example of this is eliminating subscriptions and not buying books. Instead, use the local library or free internet sites for information. What helps this exercise is a review of convenience purchases. We often buy out of convenience instead of buying on value. Another tip to reduce the pain is to calculate how much the savings will grow, so that you can see how the short-term expense reduction can allow you to spend so much more freely in the future.

Step Four. I mentioned in the last chapter the idea of creating a "savings category" where you would budget your savings. The concept is to "pay yourself first" and force a desired savings amount. While this may cause some short-term discomfort as you live on a smaller budget, the longer term results can be impressive because of the "magic of" compounding interest. The idea is to trade-off short-term desires for the pleasure of a bigger long-term prize.

"Paying yourself first" means that you have an automatic withdrawal from your checking account into a savings/investment account. This automatic withdrawal would remove funds from your checking account each month and force you to accumulate funds into a separate account that is not as easy to spend.

This removal of funds from the checking account will help you resist the temptation to spend the money you might be saving from your expense reduction efforts. It provides a means of creating savings and forces you to implement your expense reduction plan. Think of it as making you wear smaller clothes after you announce you are going on a diet.

This separate account can serve as the foundation of your investment account. As this account grows you will have the opportunity to earn greater returns through a wise investment plan.

General Investing Philosophy

❖ Have a well-diversified portfolio

❖ Use index funds

❖ Dollar cost average

❖ Keep expenses low

❖ When evaluating fixed income investments consider economic conditions and interest rates

❖ Regularly monitor your investments

Chapter Three – Wiser Investment Choices

"Why is the man (or woman) who invests all your money called a broker?" – George Carlin

"How do you make a million in the stock market? Start with two." - Anonymous

Is the stock market investing or gambling? Can you really become a millionaire through real estate like the infomercial says? If gold is such a good investment, then why does it have to be advertised so much? Inquiring minds want to know!

My thoughts on investing have been honed through my work with the ultra-wealthy. In my opinion a good investment plan has six fundamental themes:

1. Be diversified
2. Index funds are a great foundation
3. Pay attention to commissions and other expenses
4. Dollar cost average
5. Adjust your plan to economic conditions
6. Regularly review your plan

The first investment theme I would like to explore is simple diversification. This idea translates the saying, "don't put all your eggs into one basket" into a financial reality.   The suggestion is to have investments in a variety of areas so that if one area does well you participate in the gain, but if an area does poorly, then you reduce your losses by only having a portion of your investments in that particular area.

The most common method of diversification is having stocks, bonds or fixed income (which can include CDs, etc), and "hard assets" (like gold or real estate). Your stock portfolio can be further diversified by having U.S. stocks and international stocks or by having stocks of different sized companies (large, medium, and small). Your bonds or fixed income portfolio can be diversified by having U.S. and international bonds. Bonds can also be diversified by the time period in which they mature by having short-term, medium-term, and longer-term bonds.

Alternative investments like gold and real estate also offer diversification and are also available through mutual funds. A portion of your portfolio in commodities or other hard assets may make sense for many investors. These alternative investments can perform quite well in "rough" economic times and in times of inflation.

The second theme is the use of index funds. Index mutual funds are considered "passive" meaning they "track" an index that has been established. For example the Dow is an index which is the largest thirty companies in the U.S. There are index mutual funds that buy these thirty companies and then allow an investor to buy one mutual fund share. This single share represents an ownership interest in all 30 stocks.

Through index mutual funds an investor can easily diversify their investments using less than a handful of mutual funds. Using index funds, an investor can quickly diversify their portfolio into domestic and international stocks, commodities, real estate, and bonds that mature over a varied time horizon. Each mutual fund can hold hundreds and even thousands of stocks and bonds that give an investor the needed diversification.

Other mutual funds are considered to be "active". This means that the fund buys and sells companies based on the analysis of the fund manager. Instead of trying to mirror an index, the manager tries to "beat" the index, by using their own stock selection formula. Unfortunately, research has shown that most actively managed funds do not "beat" the indexes. And those who do "beat" the index may only do so for a short time.

The bottom line is that it makes sense to invest a large portion of your stock portfolio in index mutual funds. They provide diversification and are hard to "beat".

The third theme is having low investment expenses. By buying investments that have low expenses, there is more money working and compounding for you and your family. The idea of investing with index mutual funds with a low expense ratio is very appealing. All index mutual funds are not created equal. Some index mutual funds are more expensive than others, even though they offer basically the same investments. The reason for this discrepancy is the profit motive of the mutual fund or if a sales charge is added to the fund to pay a broker. A sales charge is added to many index and actively managed funds (sometimes over three percent) because the broker or financial advisor wants to get paid for their advice. Unfortunately many investors do not realize that these high commissions actually reduce their gains. **That is why I created Fundamental Financial Advisors. Fundamental Financial Advisors mainly uses low-cost mutual funds and charges a low fee instead of high commissions.**

The fourth theme is dollar cost averaging. I recently went to a charity fundraiser and at the end of the program, the charity director asked his audience to give to the charity. His words were, "Give early and give often." This mantra can also be used for the basis of your investment plan.

Dollar cost averaging is an investment technique of buying a fixed dollar amount of a particular investment on a regular schedule, regardless of the share price. More shares are purchased when prices are low, and fewer shares are bought when prices are high. The power from this approach is that it helps take emotions out of investment decisions and helps investors take a longer-term point of view. Dollar-cost averaging is a consistent approach and it helps you develop mental toughness during down markets and avoid overbuying during up markets. And it's easy to use - you can arrange to do it through automatic investment services.

The fifth theme is responding to economic conditions. When investing in bonds or other income producing investments, we want to reduce interest rate risk. An example of interest rate risk is that you buy a bond that pays 5% and then interest rates rise, and the value of your investment decreases. My philosophy is to look at the economic environment (including interest rates) and then determine what type of maturity (short-term, or longer term) I will buy. If my analysis of the economy makes me think interest rates will rise, then I will use shorter-term bond funds. If I expect interest rates to fall I will buy longer-term bond funds.

To understand the interest rate environment, one needs to monitor the macro-economic environment. A review of the world economy should occur at least monthly. **Fundamental Financial Advisors writes a monthly newsletter that reviews the macro-economic environment and the impact on investments**.

The sixth investment theme is regularly reviewing your plan. On a regular basis, investments should be reviewed and the following questions should be asked:

- o Is the investment plan producing the expected returns?

- o Are there any opportunities to take advantage of?

- o Is any particular investment category likely to be negatively or positively influenced by the economy?

- o Is now a good time to reduce investments in stocks or a time to buy more?

- o Do any of the mutual funds need to be changed based on macro-economic analysis?

o Does the dollar-cost averaging timetable need to change? Does the timetable need to be lengthened or shortened?

A regular review can be used to answer these questions, as well as determine if you need to re-balance your portfolio. When your investments grow at different rates due to your diversification, your investment portfolio needs to be re-balanced on a regular basis. For example, if your investment plan called for a fifty-fifty split between the value of stocks and bonds, and then stocks perform really well. Then the value of stocks would be greater than the value of bonds, causing a need to re-balance the portfolio to get back to a fifty-fifty split in value.

Every person's investment plan should be unique to a person's risk and financial situation. However, these six fundamental investment themes can be a part of most investment plans.

Keys to Lifelong Financial Planning

❖ Develop lifestyle and retirement goals

❖ Estimate your income, expenses, and resulting net worth to determine if you "have enough"

❖ Identify needed actions

❖ Consider term insurance

Chapter Four: Lifelong Financial Planning

"Money can't buy happiness, but it helps you look for it in more places." – Anonymous

"The question isn't at what age I want to retire, it's at what income." – George Foreman

Creating financial peace or at least worrying less about money can possibly occur with the completion of a few analyses. One of the best ways to worry less is to understand the total financial picture. My definition of the total financial picture is the understanding of income, expenses, and resulting net worth for every year you expect to be alive. If the analysis reveals that you have "enough" net worth, then your worries decline.

On the other hand, if the analyses reveal that you do not have "enough", then you will need to make plans to save more. The idea is to determine how much you need to save to give you the lifestyle you desire throughout your life.

This planning exercise can be completed in four steps:

1. Determine your lifestyle and retirement goals.
2. Estimate your living expenses, income, and resulting net worth for the rest of your life.
3. Identify needed actions.
4. Re-evaluate insurance needs

One of the first steps in this planning exercise is to determine your lifestyle and retirement goals. Questions to ask yourself about your lifestyle goals include:

- o How much (what percentage) of your children's education would you like to fund?

- At what age would you like to work for fun, rather than need to work to meet expenses?

- How much (in total for each child) would you like to give your children as an inheritance? Would you like to give them some of their inheritance before you die (if yes, when?)?

- What type of weddings do you envision for your children?

- What will your vacations be like?

- How much time or financial commitment do you envision regarding the care of your parents as they get older?

- Are there other careers/jobs that you would like to pursue? Will this increase or decrease your financial potential?

- Do you believe that you may want to continue your own formal education? If yes, when and where could you see yourself?

- What are your thoughts regarding spending on cars, boats, jewelry, or other "big ticket" items?

- What are your goals for giving to charities?

The point of these questions is to link your thoughts about how you would like to live to the impact on your financial situation. It may be advantageous for you to separate your life into two lives (pre-retirement and post-retirement) when you are answering these questions. In order to better estimate the cash flows post-retirement we ask additional questions similar to these:

- Where do you want to live when you retire?

- How will your standard of living change?

- What trips do you want to take?

- How much do you want to support your children and grandchildren?

- How much of your expenses will Social Security and your retirement plans cover?

- How well are you prepared for a long-term care need?

Step two is estimating the expenses associated with the answers to these questions, as well as your expected income and resulting net worth. At one time financial planners estimated future retirement expenses as a percentage of current expenses. I am more oriented to estimating future financial expenses based on your desires and by answering questions like the ones listed above. The idea is to estimate your living expenses during your retirement by envisioning what you want to do and estimating the costs associated with your intended lifestyle.

Once these retirement estimates are calculated and the income, expenses, and resulting net worth are estimated for each year of your life, then a planning session is in order.

The financial forecasting of a person's income, expenses, and resulting net worth can be a valuable exercise that can result in a more focused determination to improve their financial situation. Your financial advisor may have some sophisticated software that can help you with this forecast. **Fundamental Financial Advisors uses state-of-the-art technology to help with this process.**

In step three a planning session is conducted. The goal of the planning session is to determine the needed actions to ensure you will "have enough" financial resources to accomplish your goals. A review of the financial impact of your lifestyle and retirement goals can result in a variety of outcomes:

o A need to reassess your goals. Often a few reasonable
   sounding goals can result in a large financial need. For
   example, I had one client who wanted to retire at age
   sixty, pay for the education of his younger children, and
   give each child a reasonable amount of inheritance when
   they were thirty-five. Each goal in itself made sense and
   did not seem extravagant. However, when we estimated
   the financial impact and the resulting expenses for each of
   the client's future years, we realized that the goals could
   not be accomplished unless the client increased his
   salary. The result of the planning session was a slight
   modification of the client's goals. An example of this
   modification was that the client was going to work for two
   more years than he originally planned before he retired.

o A need to make some income enhancements. In the
   example above, the client not only slightly modified his
   goals, but took steps to increase his income. The client
   did not want to give up on his goals; therefore he
   developed a plan that would help him attain his financial
   dream.

o A feeling of relief when you realize your goals are
   attainable. Another client was a widowed senior citizen
   who had been retired for some time. After developing the
   estimated income and expenses for the rest of her life, we
   concluded that she "had enough" financial resources to
   meet her goals and did not have to be preoccupied with
   any worry that she may not have enough financial
   resources.

o More determination. With your financial impact of your
   goals calculated, clients can have a better understanding
   of "what it will take" to make their financial dreams a
   reality. They then have more of a determination to
   accomplish their goals.

On another note, the forecasting exercise may reveal that the identified financial gaps may take some time to eliminate. For example, a young couple may realize that they will not be able to attain their desired lifestyle for at least ten or so years. While this type of situation can provide clarity for a couple, it also reveals the need for insurance.

In step four, the task is to analyze your insurance needs. If something happened to one of the couple, then the financial dreams they had planned on often would not be fulfilled. Insurance proceeds can be included in the forecast to reveal the impact of an early death. This estimation of the impact of insurance makes the original financial projection even more robust. By analyzing the impact of an early death on the forecasted income and expenses, you may see the need to change your current insurance.

Fundamental Financial Advisors often recommends term insurance. Term insurance will allow a client to have the insurance protection at a lower cost than other forms of insurance. It can also be bought for only the time where there could be financial devastation.

Finally, this exercise of forecasting your income, expenses and resulting net worth should be completed each year. Your dreams change, life has both good and bad surprises, and your financial situation can be different after twelve months. An annual check-up for attaining your financial goals can result in you modifying your actions and "fine-tuning" your approach to fulfilling your financial dreams.

Keys to Monitoring and Updating

❖ Actual spending versus budget reviews can be enlightening

❖ A diversified portfolio will need to be "re-balanced"

❖ Economic events may impact investment plans

❖ Need to regularly "fine tune" your lifetime plan

Chapter Five: Monitoring and Updating Your Plan

"The market may be bad, but I slept like a baby last night. I woke up every hour and cried." – Anonymous

Things happen. Life is unpredictable. Therefore, I am a believer in regular reviews.

While an annual planning review will be more comprehensive, a review every three or four months would be appropriate to discuss:

- o Budget versus actual spending results

- o Actual versus planned savings levels

- o Actual investment portfolio diversification versus goals

- o Economic issues and their impact on your investment plan

As we mentioned in chapter one, a review of your spending versus budget by spending category can serve as a "fact base" to brainstorm cost cutting ideas. By the time of the first review, you have developed savings goals and lifelong financial goals. You have a better understanding of how a postponement of spending today can positively effect your future net worth. Therefore your motivation to reduce today's more frivolous spending and become more frugal should be high. Remember the goal is not to be cheap, but to be frugal and reduce the frivolous purchases. When you review your spending versus budget reports ask yourself:

- o Are my spending habits consistent with my longer-term goals?

o   Are there any expenses where a substitution of a less expensive brand would make sense?

o   Are there any spending categories that can be purchased less often?

o   What spending can I eliminate?

Have you ever seen the carnival game where you are using a play hammer to hit some stuffed animal as it pops out of a hole? In this game just as you hit one stuffed animal, another "pops up". Spending less on one category can result in moving the spending to something else. While you are reducing some purchases, other purchases maintain your overall spending levels. That is why the savings goal should also be monitored. Every few months you should monitor your deposits into your savings or investment account. The actual savings amount should be compared to your savings plan. The idea is to understand if you are meeting your goals and how you can ensure that the savings goal will be met over the next few months.

As we mentioned in chapter three, a diversified investment portfolio often needs to be re-balanced between the investment categories. Every few months your existing portfolio should be analyzed to see if it remains "close" to your targeted diversification.

Economic changes appear to be occurring at a more rapid pace. The world seems to be growing smaller as an economic event in a far-away place can affect the stock price of a local company. The need to review changes in the world economy is becoming more important. Economic changes should be reviewed in order to see if any changes need to be made to the investment plan.

Besides a review every three or four months, a more in-depth review should occur each year. In this annual review, you should ask about how your life has changed in the last year and what effect these changes have on your future financial situation. Questions could include:

- o Have any personal situations caused a need to re-think your financial plan?
    - o Any new children? Grandchildren?
    - o Any new marriages in the family?
    - o Changes in parent support?
    - o Changes in employment/promotion?

- o Have your longer-term financial goals changed?

- o Has your net worth changed in an unexpected way?

- o Have your debt levels changed and do they still make sense?

- o Do you continue to believe your forecasted income levels are accurate?

In the annual review you should also recalculate your lifetime income, expense, and resulting net worth analysis. Then take the time to see what new actions need to be implemented to best pursue your goals.

At this time you may also want to create a new budget that reflects your actual spending as well as your needed savings goals. Developing a budget after you have re-calculated your lifetime plan can make a lot of sense. The lifetime plan can bring some context on your needed savings goals which will then affect your budget priorities.

Regular reviews as well as a more in-depth annual review can help you keep your financial plan on track. These reviews should result in modifications to your actions that will better help you achieve your financial goals.

Why Consider Fundamental Financial
Advisors
(314) 567-3700
www.myfundamentaladvisor.com

☑ Customized personal budget

☑ Automatic savings plan

☑ Comprehensive investment plan

☑ Lifelong financial planning

☑ Regular monitoring and updates

☑ Easy to work with, caring attitude

☑ <u>All at an affordable cost!</u>

The Final Word

Wealth planning is an important topic and deserves your time.

However, while wealth is an important topic and wealth can do much good for the world, it is not The Truth.

No one gets off the planet alive. Besides finances, are you and your family prepared for your Godly inheritance? If your answer is not immediate, I would be delighted to talk with you or refer you to a qualified pastor.

"For God so loved the world that he gave his only Son, that whoever believes in him should not perish but have eternal life" (John 3:16)

About the author

Fess Crockett is President of Fundamental Financial Advisors (www.myfundamentaladvisor.com) and 4-C Personal Wealth Management Consultants (www.4-cwealth.com). He has an MBA in Finance from Wharton Business School and a BA in Economics from Davidson College.

He has written the book "How To Create A Wealth Plan That Works For You" and has been published by MIT's Sloan Management Review.

.